Building Your House on the Lord

by Steve & Dee Brestin

15 studies on marriage
and parenthood

Harold Shaw Publishers
Wheaton, Illinois

In this studyguide Scripture portions are quoted from
a number of different translations. The following
abbreviations are used:

JB—The Jerusalem Bible
JBP—J. B. Phillips' paraphrase
KJV—The King James Version
LB—The Living Bible
NASV—The New American Standard Version
RSV—The Revised Standard Version
TEV—Today's English Version

Library of Congress Catalog Card Number:
76-43127
ISBN 0-87788-098-0

Printed in the United States of America

contents

INTRODUCTION

WHY WAS THIS STUDYGUIDE WRITTEN?

This studyguide was written to help those of you who are in earnest about being successful in your marriage and parenthood.

The secular world offers countless books of advice on this subject. Much of this advice is based on human philosophy. To follow it is to build your house with hay and stubble. The psalmist tells us that unless the Lord builds the house, those who build it labor in vain.

Christian books, if read with discernment, often give helpful advice on marriage and parenthood. However, no book can come near to the strength and truth of God's Word. This studyguide was written to help you to build your house upon the strong wisdom of the Lord.

"For no other foundation can anyone lay than that which is laid. Now if any one builds on the foundation with gold, silver, precious stones, wood, hay, stubble—each man's work will become manifest; for the Day will disclose it, because it will be revealed with fire, and the fire will test what sort of work each one has done. If the work which any man has built on the foundation survives, he will receive a reward (I Cor. 3:11-14, RSV.) We believe you cannot apply God's word too seriously to your marriage and to the raising of your children. So, come, discover how to build your house upon the Lord!

WHAT METHOD IS USED IN THIS STUDYGUIDE?

This is an *inductive* study which means that your group will learn what the Bible says and means by asking questions which open up discussion about the Bible text itself. Certain notes on background and comments from Bible scholars are also included for added insight.

Most of the lessons in this studyguide are based on one to three passages of Scripture. This is preferable to discussing scattered scripture for two reasons. First, there is less danger of distorting the meaning of a verse when it is kept in context. Second, you will be able to remember and to refer to these basic passages in the future. Because this study is so applicable to your life, we felt this to be very important.

WHO SHOULD USE THIS STUDYGUIDE?

Individuals, couples, groups of men or women will all find this guide helpful. Both the beginning and the more seasoned student will profit from it. The beginning student will be exposed frequently to the plan of salvation and will be encouraged to find the Bible relevant to everyday living. The older Christian will be encouraged to live a Spirit-controlled life and will see familiar passages of Scripture in a new light as they are specifically applied to marriage and parenthood.

BIBLE STUDY SUGGESTIONS

POINTERS FOR ALL GROUP MEMBERS

In preparation:

1/Use a good basic translation such as the Revised Standard, the New American Standard, or the New Jerusalem Bible. If you are not a beginner and are accustomed to the King James version, you may use that. The King James translation has the advantage of being widely known and quoted. It has the disadvantage of old-fashioned grammatical forms. Paraphrases (such as *The Living Bible* and Phillips') may be used as well, but may confuse you if you try to use either of them as your basic study Bible.

2/In prayer, ask the Lord for His wisdom before you begin your study. He promises to give it if you ask (James 1:5)! Also, when you pray, ask the Lord to show you what He has for you personally in the passage to be studied. The goal of this study is *changed lives!*

3/Pray for the other group members by name every day. You'll be drawn closer to them and you need each others' prayers. In order to apply these ideal scriptural standards to our homes, we need to be abiding in Christ and living Spirit-controlled lives. So pray for your brothers and sisters!

4/Read the Scripture passages and study the questions before you come to the discussion. You will get more out of it and be a greater blessing to the others. It's also a good idea to form the habit of spending time in the Bible every day. If you haven't prepared your lesson, don't stay away from the group meeting but curb your tongue.

In discussion:

5/Even if you are a quiet beginner or just a naturally quiet person, what you have to share is important. If a thought comes into your head and your heart is beating hard, it may be that the Holy Spirit is prompting you to speak! Obey Him!

6/In each study you will find one or more "Think About It" questions. These are designed to apply to your own heart and life the principles you are discovering in the Bible. They are for personal reflection and decision rather than for group discussion.

7/If you are more advanced or naturally talkative, deliberately discipline yourself to give shyer members a chance to contribute. Discussions concerning family life can easily get out of hand. Think before you speak. Ask yourself, "Is this comment or story really going to be of help to the others?" If the Spirit tells you it won't and to be silent, obey Him!

8/As you read and discuss, questions that are "off the subject" will undoubtedly come to mind. This is especially true if this is your first Bible study. Usually, it's best not to disrupt the group with these questions but to ask someone later. There is one definite exception to this rule: if you are beginning to wonder what a real Christian is, and how to become one, be sure to ask.

POINTERS FOR THE DISCUSSION LEADER[1]

1/The best discussion leader is not a teacher but a moderator. The real teacher is the Holy Spirit and you, the human leader, must not get in His way. You should talk sparingly. If a group member asks you a question, throw it back to the group. If the question is off the subject, weed it out— gently, but firmly.

2/Your group may be quiet and slow to respond in the beginning sessions. It's better to pray silently with a smile on your face until the Holy Spirit prompts someone to answer than to get impatient and answer the question yourself! The silences may seem long—but they will lead to rewarding insights.

3/In order to draw out shyer members or to quiet talkative ones, you might ask, "Can we hear from someone who hasn't spoken up yet?" or, "What does someone else think?" Be sensitive to everyone in the group. They will enjoy the study more and learn better if they participate.

4/You should be prepared to explain how a person becomes a Christian.

Familiarize yourself with the basic elements so that you are able to pre-
sent the plan of salvation simply and clearly. The following is one
presentation:

a) God created man and desires fellowship with him. He loves man and
wants him to have an abundant life (John 10:10).

b) Man disobeyed God and went his own way; fellowship was broken
(Isaiah 53:6; Romans 3:23).

c) Jesus paid the price for sin when He died on the cross. He therefore
became the only link by which man can be restored to fellowship with
God (I Peter 3:18; John 14:6).

d) You can apply this truth personally by trusting Jesus (Revelation
3:20; John 1:12). You can do this by: repenting (confessing and forsaking sin), believing Jesus died for you, and inviting Him into your life
as your Savior and Lord.

5/Praying for one another is an important part of Christian fellowship.
In the first meeting, suggest simple prayers of thanksgiving; in your
second meeting, ask each person to pray for the person on his right;
in your third meeting, the group may progress into conversational
prayer.[2]

6/The subject of marriage and parenthood has great appeal. Encourage
your group members to be inviting friends and neighbors throughout
the study. Be sure you always have extra studyguides on hand.

SUGGESTIONS FOR THE FIRST SESSION:

1/If this is a new group, plan a ten minute get-acquainted period. You
might choose one of the following questions for each member to answer.

a) Where did you grow up and what is one of your most vivid memories
about that place?

b) Tell something about yourself and your family. What do you hope to
gain from this study?

c) What quality about your husband or wife drew you to him or her
initially? What qualities are you going to tell your children to look for in

10

a marital partner?

2/If possible, pass out the studyguide a week before your first meeting and assign the first lesson.

3/If this is not possible, you can do the first lesson together at the first meeting. Then assign the second lesson for the second meeting.

[1]*For a detailed treatment of the techniques of inductive Bible study, leaders and group members should refer to* It's Alive, the dynamics of group study, *by Gladys Hunt (Harold Shaw Publishers).*

[2]*See Rosalind Rinker's* Conversational Prayer, *Zondervan Publishing House.*

THE FOUNDATION

Read Psalm 127:1-2

1/How does the psalmist describe the work of those who build their house apart from the Lord? Will long hours and hard toil bring any lasting benefits if the Lord is not at work on your "house"?

_____

_____

2/Some marriages fail in spite of earnest effort. Some children "drop out" in spite of time spent with them. Do you know people who fit this description? What is needed in addition to time and effort to build a successful home?

_____

_____

Read Matthew 7:24-27

3/According to this passage from Matthew, if you build your house upon the sand of this world, what will happen when the storms come? What are some specific ways a home built upon Jesus and His Word would be different from a home built upon the sand of this world?

_____

_____

4/Some individuals and some families that are not building on Christ seem to be getting through life with a fair amount of order and happiness. People who are familiar with Christian principles and practice them will have happier lives. However, if they have never received Jesus Christ as their Savior and Lord, what will happen to them after death? (See I John 5:11-12.)

_____

note: I Corinthians 3:11 states: "For no other foundation can any one lay than that which is laid, which is Jesus Christ." (RSV)

"THINK ABOUT IT" QUESTION

5/Have you personally begun building your life on the rock by repenting of your sins and receiving Jesus? If this has happened to you, tell the group how it happened.

_____

6/If you have founded your life upon Jesus and are obeying Him, there is no reason for you to be anxious. According to the second verse of Psalm 127, what does God give the one He loves?

_____

7/Have you stopped toiling anxiously and begun resting in the Lord? If so, share briefly the effect this transition has had in one specific area of your life.

_____

8/Anyone who has Jesus as his foundation will be saved. However, some Christians mature faster and experience more of the abundant life than other Christians. Their homes reflect this maturity, and their marriage partner and their children are blessed by it. Meditate on I Cor. 3:12-15, *The Living Bible.*

What does it mean to build with "gold, silver and jewels? Does this kind of building take more planning, time and work than a building of sticks and straw? What is the value of building with silver and gold?

_____

_____

*note: When you tell your children the story of "The Three Little Pigs"
consider the spiritual application. The wolf is coming to huff and to puff!
and some will be left with only a foundation!*

Read Psalm 127:3-5

9/These verses explain the blessings children bring to a home. Why is it
best to have your home founded on the Lord before children arrive?

_____

*note: Many parents commit their lives to the Lord long after their chil-
dren have arrived. They should go to their children and confess that they
have built their home on the wrong foundation. They need to ask their
forgiveness and tell them they are now going to build on Christ and His
Word. Such repentance (confessing and forsaking sin) is a tremendous
witness.*

10/How should your recognition that children are God's gift influence
your attitude toward them?

_____

_____

11/To what does the psalmist compare children in verses 3-5? Why is
their father happy?

_____

_____

12/What is the most important thing a parent can teach his child? Why?
How can parents best go about teaching their family to build their lives
on the Lord?

_____

_____

_____

2

Understanding God's Blueprint for:
MARRIAGE—BEFORE THE FALL

Read Genesis 2:18-20

1/In the creation account, God repeatedly observes that what He has brought into being "was good". Now, for the first time in Genesis 2:18 God says "It is not good". What was not good? What does this tell you about our basic human make-up?

_____

_____

note: Man is lonely without woman (and vice-versa). This does not mean, however, that everyone should marry. (This topic will be covered in lesson 8.)

2/God said He would make a "help meet" or a "helper fit" for the man. This means, literally, "a help answering to him". The Lord made woman very different from man. She complements his nature as he does hers and together they make a stronger unit than would two persons of the same sex. Describe some differences between you and your spouse that allow you to complement each other.

_____

_____

"THINK ABOUT IT" QUESTION

3/Take a moment of quiet and ask the Lord to direct your thoughts and show you one or two specific ways you can better meet the needs of your spouse this week. What is it that the Lord has shown you to do?

note: In today's world there is an increasing emphasis on putting our own needs first. It is important to understand why this is contrary to God's plan. Again and again in this study you will see that we are to put another's needs first—which really means to be in submission to each other.

Read Genesis 2:21-23 with Ephesians 5:28, 29

4/Woman was made from man. She is "bone of his bones and flesh of his flesh". How should this knowledge influence a man's attitude toward his wife?

Read Genesis 2:24

note: This is one of the most important verses on marriage in God's Word. It is repeated four times in the New Testament.

5/What is the result of the truth of verse 23 (note the word "therefore" which joins verses 23, 24)?

"THINK ABOUT IT" QUESTION

6/In family relationships, does your spouse come first? Does he (or she) come before your parents? Before your children? If your answer is yes, can you give some evidence to support it?

7/What do you think God means when he tells marriage partners to "Leave their parents?" Does this ever mean abandonment?

8/In many countries, a newly married couple moves in with one set of parents. Do you think it is possible to leave parents emotionally but not physically? On the other hand, do you think it is possible for a couple to leave physically but not emotionally?

_____

_____

9/How should the knowledge that a married couple must eventually "leave" their parents influence your attitude toward your children when they marry? How will you apply this now, before their marriage?

_____

_____

10/The literal meaning of the Hebrew word for "to cleave" is "to stick to—to be glued together". If you pull apart two pieces of paper that are glued together, they will both be torn. In light of this, why is the marriage bond so serious?

_____

_____

note: "Cleaving means love . . . of a special kind. It is love which has made a decision and which is no longer a groping and seeking love. Love which cleaves is mature love, love which has decided to remain faithful –faithful to one person–and to share with this one person one's whole life."[1]

11/If you have decided to cleave to your marital partner, how should that decision influence your thoughts and decisions if someone else very attractive comes along?

_____

_____

note: After you "leave" and "cleave", you become one flesh. You unite with your partner physically, emotionally, and spiritually. You are no longer two, but one. Notice this melding step comes last.

12/How does the knowledge that God instituted marriage as a serious commitment influence your perspective toward your own marriage?

[1]*Walter Trobisch*, I Married You, *1971, Harper & Row, p. 16. Used by permission of the author.*

3

Understanding God's blueprint for:
MARRIAGE—AFTER THE FALL

Read Genesis 3:1-6

1/In verse 1, how did Satan cause doubt in Eve's mind? How does Satan cause doubt in our minds concerning God's Word today?

_____

_____

_____

2/To what weakness in Eve did Satan appeal in verse 5? Give an example of how this same weakness might keep a person from hearing and applying God's Word today.

_____

_____

Read Genesis 3:7-13

3/In response to God's question (verse 11), whom did Adam blame? When God questioned Eve, whom did she blame? Who is to blame for your sin?

_____

note: Secular marriage counselors often blame a failing marriage on one or more of the partner's parents. When you come to Christ you are a new creation and your background is no longer an excuse for your behavior. You have His Holy Spirit and therefore you have the power to change and to be healed of even the psychological scars of a difficult childhood.

4/Eve had not been created when God gave the command to not eat of the tree of the knowledge of good and evil. Did God still hold her accountable? Who was responsible for telling her of God's command? Do you see any significance in these facts?

_____

_____

_____

Read Genesis 3:14-15

5/What curse did God pronounce upon the serpent in verse 14?

_____

note: Verse 15 is a famous passage. In the midst of this account of the fall and its consequences God gives the first prophesy of His solution. This is "called the protevangelium, 'first gospel,' the announcement of a prolonged struggle, perpetual antagonism, wounds on both sides, and eventual victory for the seed of woman. God's promise that the head of the serpent was to be crushed pointed forward to the coming of the Messiah and guaranteed victory."[1]

Read Genesis 3:16-19

6/God revised his blueprint for husbands and wives because of sin. List the changes the fall brought into our lives. (verses 16-19)

_____

_____

_____

7/According to verse 16, does pain in childbirth take away a woman's desire for her husband? In what ways does a woman "desire" her husband?

_____

_____

8/God's purpose for the wife was for her to be a helper suitable to her husband and to have children. God's purpose for the husband was for him to work for a living. The world is rebelling at these traditional roles, calling them "stereotypes." Should Christians join the rebellion? Why or why not?

_____

_____

9/Do you think it is possible for a Christian to exaggerate these roles into lines God didn't intend? Explain—and support your answer scripturally if you can.

_____

_____

10/Both men and women often feel that the pressure of their role in life is too much for them. What or who is our resource in our inadequacy?

_____

note: Jesus says, in Matthew 11:28-30: "Come to me, all who labor and are heavy laden, and I will give you rest. Take my yoke upon you, and learn from me; for I am gentle and lowly in heart, and you will find rest for your soul. For my yoke is easy, and my burden is light." (RSV)

"THINK ABOUT IT" QUESTION

11/Have you come to Jesus? Has He given you rest? How has He lightened your load and made your life worth living?

_____

_____

_____

[1]From The Wycliffe Bible Commentary, Moody Press, 1962, p. 8.

4

Building with God's basic instructions for:
THE BELIEVER'S WALK

Read Ephesians 5:1-2

1/What is the command in verse 2? What does it mean? What example are we given?

_____

_____

2/Give some specific examples of how you might "walk in love" toward your husband or wife. In a Bible study group, how should members walk in love toward each other?

_____

_____

_____

3/Verse 2 states that Jesus showed His love for us by giving Himself for us as a sacrifice to God. What was the purpose of Jesus' death on the cross (See II Corinthians 5:21)? Many believe this truth intellectually. What must any individual do to apply Jesus' sacrifice to the heart as well as to the head?

_____

_____

4/Have you repented and received Jesus as your Savior and Lord? If so, has this changed your life? Has it changed your marriage? How?

_____

_____

_____

Read Ephesians 5:3-10

5/Summarize the kind of behavior and conversation that is unfitting for the believer. Why is it unfitting?

_____

_____

_____

note: The Greek verbs in verse 4 connote vulgar and coarse jesting (what we might call "dirty jokes"). Paul Little offers this advice to the Christian who gets caught in a room where off-color stories are being told: "Be alert for the first lull in conversation and then jump in with a good clean story. Tell one so funny that people can't help laughing. . . . By the grace of God we can, without compromising ourselves or condoning his words, respond with love to the one who swears or tells off-color stories."[1]

6/Why should Christians have a sense of humor? (Perhaps your family could practice some good, clean, funny stories at the dinner table tonight.)

_____

7/A Christian family can be a haven from the storm of the world. What are some specific ways you might strengthen your spouse or children for their encounters with secular pressures?

_____

_____

8/The Greek noun in verse 7 means "partaker". Check your dictionary. What does "partake" mean? In what should a believer *not* partake? Pornography and astrology are two examples of activities of darkness—

what are some others? What reason is given for not partaking in these (verses 8-9)?

_____

_____

_____

"THINK ABOUT IT" QUESTION

9/The RSV translates verse 10: "And try to learn what is pleasing to the Lord." How can you go about doing this?

_____

_____

Read Ephesians 5:11-17

10/J. B. Phillips paraphrases verse 11: "Steer clear of the activities of darkness; let your lives show by contrast how dreary and futile these things are." Can you think of a specific example of how a Christian family's way of life might show this contrast to the world?

_____

_____

11/Why should we walk wisely and carefully (verses 15-17)? Have you ever lost time because you acted impulsively without seeking the Lord's guidance?

_____

_____

note: Laziness or indifference may prevent us from actively seeking the Lord's will or obeying it. This is building life with "hay and stubble." It's a shortcut–but the work won't endure because the foundation of God's plan and blessing is missing.

12/Why is it especially important for Christian parents to "walk in love" (verse 2), "walk in light" (verse 8), and walk carefully and wisely (verse

15) during their child-raising years?

_____

_____

[1]Taken from How to Give Away Your Faith by Paul Little. © 1962 by Inter-Varsity Christian Fellowship and used by permission of InterVarsity Press.

5

Building with God's basic instructions for:
THE BELIEVER'S WALK IN MARRIAGE

Read Ephesians 5:18-21

1/To whom is this passage addressed (Eph. 5:1)?

2/What should stimulate and control a believer? What should not? Some Christians are so filled with the Spirit that you can tell that they know the Lord as soon as you meet them. Have you ever met someone like this? Describe him/her.

---

note: Being continually filled with the Spirit and learning to walk in the Spirit is the key to a blessed marriage and home.

3/What is the difference between walking in the flesh and walking in the Spirit (See Romans 8:5-8)?

---

note: Romans continues with a description of the Spirit-filled walk: "Nevertheless once the Spirit of him who raised Christ Jesus from the dead lives within you he will, by that same Spirit, bring to your whole being new strength and vitality. So then, my brothers, you can see that we have no particular reason to feel grateful to our sensual nature, or to live life on the level of the instincts. Indeed that way of living leads to certain spiritual death. But if on the other hand you cut the nerve of your instinctive actions by obeying the Spirit, you are on the way to real living." Romans 8:11-13 (JBP)

4/When Christ lives in you, so does the Holy Spirit. How does a person receive Christ (Revelation 3:20)? With this "picture" in mind, tell how a person continues to be filled with the Spirit (Be sure to hear from several members of the group.)

_____

_____

note: Tim LaHaye points out the importance of confessing and forsaking sin, which grieves the Holy Spirit. " 'How often should you ask to be filled with the Spirit?' is a question I am frequently asked. My answer is, 'Every time you are conscious you are not filled.' Ephesians 5:18 makes it clear that we should be continually in the process of being filled with His Spirit." [1]

5/In verse 19 what is the result of being continually Spirit-filled? Does this verse describe your home's atmosphere? Do you listen to a Christian radio station? Play Christian records? Does your family sing hymns and spiritual songs together?

_____

note: If we feed our spiritual nature with Christian messages and Christian music, that nature will grow. If we feed our fleshly nature with secular television programs and music, that nature will grow.

6/For what should we give thanks according to verse 20? How can a believer be thankful for trials and tribulations (See James 1:2-3)?

_____

7/What command is given in verse 21? To whom is it addressed? What does this mean? (For other Scriptures which go into detail on this subject, see I Peter 5:5 and Philippians 2:3-9.)

_____

8/Describe some specific examples of how a husband and wife could "submit one to another in the fear of God."

_____

_____

"THINK ABOUT IT" QUESTION

9/Ask the Lord to show you how you might better helpl your spouse. Has pride or selfishness kept you from really walking in love toward your husband/wife? How, specifically, will you change your attitude or behavior?

_____

Read Ephesians 5:22-33

10/What relationship does the marriage of Spirit-filled believers illustrate?

_____

11/From verses 24, 33, what attitude does the church (the "body" of all true believers) have toward Christ? What attitude should a wife have toward her husband? Can you think of several specific ways a woman could show respect and submission to her husband?

_____

_____

_____

12/Who is to be the head of the wife and home? For what responsibilities is the head of the home held accountable? (If you can support your answer scripturally, do.) Is it possible for a woman to make it difficult for her husband to be head of the home? How?

_____

_____

_____

note: Paul D. Meier, a Christian psychiatrist, notes that about 85% of mentally ill persons were raised in a home where there was a weak, passive father and a domineering, overprotective mother.[2]

13/What attitude did Christ have toward the church (verses 25-30)? What attitude should a husband have toward his wife? Can you think of several specific ways that a man could show sacrificial love to his wife? Give a brief description of a husband's Christ-like authority.

_____

_____

_____

note: Although the man is head of the home, the fact that his wife is part of him and part of the body of Christ should cause him to seriously consider her ministry, *her* needs, *her* ideas *and her* gifts.

14/Decisions ranging from buying a television to taking a new job affect the wife and often the children. How might a husband effectively seek the Lord's will for *all* of them in these decisions?

_____

_____

note: God expects a great deal in the marriage of Spirit-filled believers. This life on earth is often difficult, but He promised to help us. (See John 16:33; I Peter 5:10.) As each of us learns to obey Him we become conformed to the image of Christ.

[1]*From* How to Win Over Depression *by Tim LaHaye. Copyright © 1974 by The Zondervan Corporation. Used by permission.*
[2]*From "Is Divorce Ever Necessary?" by Paul Meier, Christian Medical Society Journal, Winter, 1976. Used by permission.*

6

I Peter 2:21–3:7

Building with God's special instructions for:
MARRIAGE IN DIFFICULT CIRCUMSTANCES: PART I

Read I Peter 2:21-25

1/When Christ suffered, He left an example for believers to follow. How did He react? In whom did He trust? In what specific ways, then, should we "follow in his steps?"

_____

_____

_____

note: Refusing to respond angrily under persecution or false accusation is easier if you consciously commit your case to the Lord. Discipline for your persecutor is His concern—not yours (See Romans 12:19).

2/Jesus' suffering was an example for us—but it was much more. What was the three-fold purpose of His crucifixion (verse 24)? Does this mean anything to you personally? Explain.

_____

_____

Read I Peter 3:1-6

note: Verse 1 begins with "In the same manner". This phrase refers us back to chapter 2 where men are instructed to submit to the ruling authority and servants to their masters as Jesus submitted to His Father.

3/To whom are wives to submit? What reason for optimism is given to wives of unbelieving husbands?

_____

_____

4/The wife of an unbelieving husband has two alternatives. What are they? Which works best? Why do you think this is? Do you think this verse could be applied to winning other unbelieving members of a household to Christ?

_____

_____

5/Some women hesitate to make a decision for Christ because they fear it will create a divided home. What would you tell them?

_____

_____

6/How do you think a woman with an unbelieving husband can avoid being weakened by him and instead grow stronger spiritually?

_____

_____

7/What kind of adornment makes a woman truly beautiful? Have you ever met a woman whose faith in Christ gave her a special beauty? Describe her.

_____

note: Compare verses 3-5 with this passage: "Likewise I want women to adorn themselves with proper clothing, modestly and discreetly, not with braided hair and gold or pearls or costly garments; but rather by means of good works, as befits women making a claim to godliness." I Timothy 2:9, 10 (NAS)

8/How do you think a woman making a claim to godliness should dress today? Are there certain things she should avoid? Why?

9/One way Sarah showed her respect for Abraham was by calling him "lord." How do you show respect for your husband? (Or how does your wife show respect for you?).

10/A woman should clearly submit to her unbelieving husband. Likewise, a servant should be subject to his master (I Peter 2:18) and a man should be subject to the ruling authority (I Peter 2:13). However, if the authority over you makes a request that clearly goes against what God commands, what should you do? What did Peter do in this circumstance? (See Acts 5:25-32.)

11/Briefly name some requests an unbelieving husband might make of his wife that would clearly go against God. How might a woman refuse gently but honestly?

note: *This is a difficult circumstance and she must truly be Spirit led. A woman should submit whenever she can, but she must remember her own accountability before God. (Romans 14:12) She cannot agree to disobey God.*

When Nabal, an unbelieving husband, determined to do wrong, his wife Abigail did not support him but worked contrary to him. The Lord took Nabal's life and blessed Abigail (I Sam. 25).

A woman must not be capricious in her submission, but she should walk carefully. She must avoid self-righteousness. She should pray as David did, "Search me, O God, and know my heart, try me, and know my thoughts; And see if there be any wicked way in me, and lead me in the way everlasting." Psalm 139:23-24 (KJV)

Read I Peter 3:7

12/Here Peter is speaking to believing husbands. He begins with the word "Likewise". He is referring again to the examples of submission given already in this letter. Obviously men are not to take advantage of their submissive wives. Is it possible for a man to be head of his home in a spirit of gentleness? Whose example is he to follow (Ephesians 5:25)? Can a man exhibit both authority and a "servant spirit" at the same time (Mark 10:43-45)?

_____

_____

_____

_____

note: J. B. Phillips paraphrases verse 7 as follows: "Similarly, you husbands should try to understand the wives you live with, honouring them as physically weaker yet equally heirs with you in the grace of life. If you don't do this, you will find it impossible to pray properly."

13/How might a husband gain a better understanding of his wife? What can a woman do to help him? Why is this important?

_____

_____

14/Most women are physically weaker than most men. How might a man show a considerate awareness of this?

_____

15/If a man abuses his position as head of the home and does not treat his wife considerately, what will happen to his communication with God?

_____

"THINK ABOUT IT" QUESTION

16/What have you as a wife/husband learned from this discussion which will make a difference in your relationship with your spouse this week?

_____

7

Building with God's special instructions for:
MARRIAGE IN DIFFICULT CIRCUMSTANCES: PART II

Read I Peter 3:8-12

1/Now Peter turns to all believers—both husbands and wives. In verse 8 he tells them to be "of one mind." How is it possible for believers to be of one mind? (See Philippians 2:2, 5 and 4:2). How might a couple develop this like-mindedness? What would its benefits be in their home?

_____

_____

_____

2/Sympathy is the next characteristic on Peter's list. Define "sympathy," using a dictionary. How does this fit in with like-mindedness?

_____

3/Peter then tells the believers to be loving and compassionate. Describe some ways in which the life of your spouse or child is difficult. How can you show special love and compassion for that person in such a circumstance? When you think of loving your "brothers," do you include spouse and children in your thoughts?

_____

_____

_____

4/Finally, in verse 8, we're told to be humble in spirit. Why is humility so important for a good marriage?

5/How should you respond to insults and thoughtless remarks (verse 9)? How did Jesus respond? (Read I Peter 2:23.)

6/The world advises us against repression, and encourages self-expression. What is the Lord's counsel in verse 10?

7/Give an example of actively seeking and pursuing peace in a marital or family situation.

8/What blessing is given to those who do the Lord's will (verse 12)? How does this echo verse 7? Is there any behavior in your life that is hindering your prayers? What should you do about it?

note: Peter, in verses 10-12, is quoting from Psalm 34. This is a beautiful and comforting passage for the believer facing difficult circumstances. You'll receive a special blessing if you meditate on it.

Read I Peter 3:13-17

note: This passage gives advice to believers in an unbelieving world. Perhaps part of that unbelieving world is in your own home, or very close to you.

9/Who is likely to harm you if you are pleasing the Lord (verse 13)? But if you are criticized how should you feel about it? (See also I Peter 4:12-14)

10/Meditate on verse 15. Here we are told to be prepared to give an answer for why we believe as we do. Prepare a gentle and respectful answer for one of the following hypothetical situations—choose the one that seems most likely for you.

a) An unbelieving spouse says, "Honey, there's really been a change in you. What's happened?"

_____

_____

b) A friend at work comments, 'I saw you reading your Bible. How can you swallow all those myths?"

_____

_____

c) A neighbor says, "I've really been having trouble with my ten year old. Your children are so well-behaved. How do you do it?"

_____

_____

d) Another neighbor comments, "I heard your husband/wife cutting you down last night and you didn't stand up for your rights. Why not, for Pete's sakes?..

_____

_____

10/Why are we told to answer gently and respectfully?

_____

12/If your life is drawing criticism and persecution, of what should you make certain (verse 16)?

_____

13/What similarities did you notice between the verses from Ephesians 5 and I Peter 3?

_____

_____

_____

"THINK ABOUT IT" QUESTION

14/What was the most meaningful part of this passsage in I Peter for you? Why?

_____

_____

8

Understanding God's view of divorce:
DEMOLITION?

note: Study 8 has been written so that those who are married will better understand God's view of divorce, not to judge those who have been divorced. (Special consideration of the problems of divorce will be given at the end of the study.) Because this is a sensitive topic it is suggested that your particular group be led by the Spirit as to whether or not this lesson should be discussed together or simply be studied privately.

Read Matthew 19:3-12

1/What was the first question the Pharisees asked Jesus (verse 3)? Read Jesus' answer carefully and paraphrase it in your own words.

_____

_____

_____

2/What was the Pharisees' second question (verse 7)?

_____

3/Why did Jesus say Moses permitted divorce? What does it mean to be "hard hearted?"

_____

_____

note: By contrast, God's way for us is: "Be ye kind one to another, tenderhearted, forgiving one another, even as God, for Christ's sake, hath forgiven you." (Ephesians 4:32 KJV)

4/Is there anything that a child of God has the right to consider unforgiveable? Why not? (Meditate on Matthew 18:21-35 for added understanding.)

_____

note: Scholars disagree on the meaning of Matthew 19:9. The usual "evangelical" stand is that adultery is the only scriptural ground for divorce. Certainly Jesus doesn't demand divorce here. He has already told us in Matthew 18:35 that we should forgive our brother every one of his trespasses. However, if a spouse is unwilling to repent of adultery and thus change his ways, the marriage is already broken in spirit. Then it does seem that the loving counsel would be to permit the wronged party a legal break in the relationship as well–that is, divorce.

5/From this passage, how do you think God views divorce?

_____

6/What was the disciples' reaction to this statement of the permanency of marriage (verse 10)? How did Jesus answer them?

_____

_____

Read Malachi 2:11-16

7/Briefly summarize the situation described here. Why is God angry with the men of Israel?

_____

_____

_____

8/How seriously had the Israelites taken their marriage vows (verse 14)? If you have made marriage vows before God, how seriously do you take them?

_____

9/How do you react to God's strong statement about divorce in verse 16?

Read I Corinthians 7:10-16

note: The world only gives the person in an unhappy marriage two alternatives: either a life of misery, or divorce. With that perspective, many people choose divorce. However, the Lord offers a better way. Two people can come to Him, study and apply His Word, and learn to develop a fulfilling and blessed marriage. Even if only one marriage partner comes, that may begin to turn the tide. The Lord sets high standards, but He is also willing to give wisdom and help to meet them.

10/Why should the believing partner stay with the unbelieving partner?

Verse 14 states that the spouse and children of a believer are sanctified or consecrated. This does not mean that they are automatically saved but that they have been set apart for special treatment. Close contact with a believer increases chances for a change in their lives.

11/Verse 10 tells the believer not to be a deserter. Then verse 11 goes on to say, "but and if she departs. . . ." God's ideal is for a person to stay with the spouse. Is the believer who does depart free to remarry?

12/According to verse 15, what should the believer do if he unbeliever wants to depart? Why?

note: There are two interpretations of the statement that a believer "not be under bondage in such cases." It may mean that the deserted believer should not be held to his marriage vows and should be free to get a divorce. Or, it may simply mean that the believer should not try to force the unbeliever to stay.

13/Does the believing partner have any guarantee that his spouse will be saved (verse 16)?

14/Has this study of God's view of divorce affected your attitude toward your marriage? What steps would you take if you felt your marriage was in trouble?

---

note: God hates divorce, but He still loves those who have been divorced. Sometimes believers seem unforgiving toward the divorced, but God always offers forgiveness. Jesus tells us all sins (including divorce!) may be forgiven except blasphemy against the Holy Spirit (continual and total rejection of the Lord–(Matthew 12:31). Donald Cole, a radio pastor, says, "... Once the papers are signed, it's too late for rebukes, too late for the good advice which, at an earlier stage, might have saved the marriage. Compassion and acceptance are needed now."–Donald Cole, "What to Say to a Divorced Friend"[1]

15/Meditate on the following passage from Philippians. "This one thing I do, forgetting those things which are behind, and reaching forth unto those things which are before, I press toward the mark for the prize of the high calling of God in Christ Jesus." Phil. 2:13, 14 (KJV). How might this passage help the divorced person?

"THINK ABOUT IT" QUESTION

16/Proverbs 17:17 says that 'A friend loveth at all times, and a brother is born for adversity." If you have divorced friends, how can you show your love and compassion for them?

Building with God's instructions for:
THE ROOT AND FRUIT OF LOVE IN THE FAMILY

note: You are midway through the study. This would be a good time to reread the pointers for study and discussion found in the Bible Study Suggestions (pages 7-10).

Read John 15:1-11

1/In this parable of Jesus, who is the vine? Who is the vinedresser? Who are the branches?

_____

_____

2/Describe the "fruit" of Christian character. (See Galatians 5:22, 23)

_____

3/When we are in public, we can usually manage to display the fruit of Christian character. It is in the home that our true character is revealed. According to verses 4 and 5, how can we *continually* bear the fruit of Christian character?

_____

_____

4/Check your dictionary and define the word "abide." What is the difference between *visiting* and *abiding*? How would you tell a person to go about abiding in Christ? How should he go about letting Christ abide in him? (One helpful passage for personal meditation on this topic is I John 1:5—2:6)

_____

_____

_____

5/According to verse 8, who is glorified when Christians bear fruit?

_____

note: When Christians truly love each other and live in unity the world notices! (See John 17:21-23) What a tremendous witness a loving Christian family gives!

6/According to verses 10 and 11, what is characteristic of the life of an obedient child of God?

_____

note: Just as obedience leads to joy, so disobedience leads to depression. The depressed believer should open himself to God's searching, confess his sin, begin again to obey, and watch his life fill up with joy!

7/When you are filled with the joy of the Lord what effect does it have on your home? When you are depressed what is the effect on your family?

_____

_____

8/Why shouldn't a Christian allow depression to go undealt with?

_____

Read I Corinthians 13:1-7

note: This passage is a description of Christ-like love. It is important to remember that the only way of exhibiting this kind of caring love is by abiding in Christ. True joy and love in a home do not result from pleasant circumstances but from abiding in Christ. If you don't have joy and love, it's a problem of your spiritual relationship with Him.

9/God gives spiritual gifts to His children. Of what profit are they if they are not exercised in love (verses 1-3)? When one serves his family without love, how worthwhile is that service to God?

_____

_____

note: The quotations in the following questions are taken from the Williams translation of I Cor. 13.

10/"Love is so patient and so kind...." Give an example from your experience of this kind of love in action, between parent and child.

_____

_____

11/"Love never boils with jealousy" Give an example of this kind of love in a wife toward her husband.

_____

_____

12/"It never boasts, is never puffed with pride; It does not act with rudeness, or insist upon its rights" Give an example of this kind of love in a husband toward his wife.

_____

_____

13/"It never gets provoked, it never harbors evil thoughts" Are you frequently provoked by your spouse or by a child? How can you change this?

_____

_____

note: One suggestion would be to take time to look at yourself rather than the "provoker". Ask the Lord to search you and to show you how to *deal with the situation. Then listen to the Lord and obey the insight He gives you!*

14/"Is never glad when wrong is done, but always glad when truth prevails." Are you willing to be proven wrong so that truth can prevail? To apologize for your mistakes?

_____

15/"It bears up under anything, it exercises faith in everything, it keeps up hope in everything, it gives power to endure anything." When does your spouse or child need your love the most—in success or failure? When does a loving relationship find its greatest opportunity to grow—during stress or tranquillity?

_____

_____

Read Revelation 2:1-5

Many couples today feel that because they "don't love each other any more," their marriage relationship should be dissolved.

16/The church at Ephesus had "fallen out of love" with Jesus. What three instructions were they given, in verse 5, to restore that first love? What could "remembering" a love relationship, "repenting" for its loss, and deliberately choosing to act in love do for a cold marriage? For tension between you and your child?

_____

_____

_____

Take a few minutes of silent prayer to begin *in your heart* to right any wrong relationships in your family. Write down any practical steps you should take in this direction.

_____

_____

10

Colossians 3:1-4
Ecclesiastes 4:9-12
Deuteronomy 6:4-9

Building with God's instructions for:
SPIRITUAL EXPRESSION IN THE FAMILY

Read Colossians 3:1-4

1/List some spiritual goals. List some typical earthly objectives. According to this passage, why should a believer in Christ be setting and seeking spiritual goals rather than earthly ones? Describe the proper focus of the believer's life.

_____

_____

_____

2/Read Matthew 6:21. In terms of daily choices and decisions, what does this verse teach us?

_____

3/List some specific ways that you could encourage yourself and your family to fill your minds and hearts with spiritual treasures? (See Colossians 3:15-17 for added insight.)

_____

_____

Read Ecclesiastes 4:9-12

4/According to this passage, what advantages might marriage have over the single life?

5/If "two are better than one," three are better than two! In verse 12, what makes a marriage partnership "threefold?" Is Christ at the head of your marriage? If so, how has He strengthened it?

_____

_____

6/If your spouse is a believer how have you been helped to be strong? Has he/she ever helped you up when you were down, spiritually? Explain.

_____

_____

7/What are some specific things you need to do to encourage _your_ spouse in the Lord?

_____

_____

8/One of the main ways we influence those close to us is by example. Paul was able to say, "those things which ye have both learned, and received, and heard, and seen in me, do...." (Philippians 4:9) If your spouse or your child models his spiritual habits after yours, will he grow closer to the Lord?

_____

Read Deuteronomy 6:4-9

9/What did the Lord teach His people, Israel, in verse 5? (Jesus repeats this in the New Testament as being the most important commandment. See Mark 12:28-34.) Paraphrase this commandment in your own words. In what ways might your life give evidence of this kind of love for the Lord?

_____

10/Meditate on verse 7. When should we be teaching our children about the Lord? What does it mean to teach "diligently"? Give examples from your experience.

11/In addition to informal spiritual conversations throughout the day, a scheduled time of family devotions can be of real value. Describe some ways that family devotions could be conducted so that they would be both rewarding and enjoyable for the following age levels:

a) Preschool

b) Elementary

c) Teenage

12/In verses 8 and 9 the Lord is telling believers to put reminders of Him and His Word everywhere! Do you have Christian symbols, posters, pictures, bulletin boards, etc. in your home? Briefly describe what you have. What is its effect on the "climate" of your household?

note: *"The story is told of a woman whose three sons, to her great disappointment, all took up the life of seafaring men. She was relating this to a visitor in the home one day, saying that she could not understand why they had all chosen to go to sea.*

'How long have you had that picture?' The visitor inquired, pointing

50

to a large painting that hung in the dining room.

'Oh, for years,' the woman replied, 'ever since the children were small.'

'There is your answer,' the visitor said. For hanging on the dining-room wall was the painting of a large sailing vessel cutting smartly through the waves, its sails at full billow, the captain standing straddle-legged on the quarter deck, his spy-glass in hand, scanning the horizon.

Morning, noon and night—with every meal—the boys had taken into their inner consciousness the sense of high adventure portrayed in that picture. Effortlessly, with never a word being spoken, it had planted in them a hankering for the sea."[1]

"THINK ABOUT IT" QUESTION

13/What is the most meaningful part of this lesson for you? Why?

_____

[1]Taken from The Christian Family, © 1970, Bethany Fellowship. Used by permission.

11

*Proverbs 5:15-21
I Corinthians 6:9–7:9*

Building with God's instructions for:
PHYSICAL EXPRESSION IN MARRIAGE

Read Proverbs 5:15-21

1/This passage is one of the really positive scriptural encouragements toward sexual expression in marriage. Some people have the idea that the Lord is against sexual enjoyment, even in marriage. From this passage, what kind of sexual activity displeases the Lord? What pleases Him?

---

note: The KJV explicitly translates verse 19: "Let her be as the loving hind and pleasant roe; let her breasts satisfy thee at all times, and be thou ravished always with her love."

2/One definition of the word "ravished" is "to be carried away with ecstasy". What positive things can a husband or wife do to keep joy and delight in their sexual relationship? (You and your spouse should discuss this privately and in detail together.)

3From this passage, does God feel you need more than one partner in a lifetime for true satisfaction?

4Secular marriage "counselors" may advise a person to participate in a clandestine extra-marital affair. What is false in this kind of thinking?

"THINK ABOUT IT" QUESTION

5/How does the knowledge that God planned and is pleased with the marital sexual relationship affect your own attitude toward it?

Read I Corinthians 6:9-20

6/What principle do verses 9, 15, and 18 echo from the passage in Proverbs?

7/Sexual sin seems to cause more guilt than other types of sin. A person who has repented (confessed and forsaken) his sin to God *can* enter into a blessed marital relationship. How does Paul describe this to us in verse 11?

---

note: *Many persons who have been unhappy in their marital physical relationship find that the situation changes when they come to Christ and claim his promise of forgiveness for their past. He has replaced their guilt and anxiety with peace and joy! Praise the Lord!*

8/A Christian's involvement with a prostitute is "an abomination" to the Lord. Why (verses 15-17)?

9/How should the knowledge that you are *part of Christ* affect what you do with your body and mind?

10/How should a Christian handle sexual temptation (verse 18)? What does this verse mean? How should you cope with sexual fantasy in your thought life? What else is important to help you avoid sexual immorality?

_____

_____

11/Verse 20 says we have been bought with a price. What was the price? How can you apply this to your life, personally?

_____

_____

Read I Corinthians 7:1-9

12/What is God's provision for both personal fulfillment and the problem of temptation?

_____

13/Meditate on verses 3 and 4. Express what Paul is saying in your own words.

_____

_____

14/Is a husband or wife who rejects the marriage partner sexually within the will of God? Why not? What is the root problem behind such rejection?

_____

_____

14/Is it possible to frequently discourage your spouse from suggesting intimacy without verbally saying "No"? How? What is the inevitable result of this subtle form of refusal and deprivation?

_____

15/God calls some people to remain single. What is one way of testing that this is his call (verse 9)?

_____

16/Some relationship principles covered in past studies are listed below. How might you specifically apply these principles to the physical relationship? (Marriage partners should discuss this in detail, privately.)

a) The Lord made men and women different. Are there some differences between you and your spouse that you should recognize and allow for in your sexual relationship?

———————————————————————————————

b) Husbands and wives should be in submission to each other—each thinking of the other's needs first. Apply this to your sexual relationship.

———————————————————————————————

c) Husbands should love their wives as their own bodies, nurturing and cherishing them. Husbands, how might you apply this in your marriage?

———————————————————————————————

d) Wives should show respect for their husbands. Wives, how might you apply this in your marriage?

———————————————————————————————

12

Building with God's instructions for:
COMMUNICATION IN THE FAMILY

Read Ephesians 4:25-32

note: You might also read Ephesians 4:17-24 in order to take in the whole context of this passage. Paul is telling believers that since they have the Holy Spirit their behavior should differ from the behavior of non-believers. One area this difference should be seen is in their communication!

1/What compelling reason for honesty is given in verse 25? Who are our closest neighbors? What effect does dishonesty have on a husband-wife relationship? On a parent-child relationship?

_____

_____

_____

2/Does speaking the truth mean we can be insensitive in our openness? What should always modify our truthfulness (Ephesians 4:15)? *The Living Bible* paraphrases I Corinthians 13:5 this way: "Love does not demand its own way. It is not irritable or touchy. It does not hold grudges and will hardly even notice when others do it wrong." In levelling with others, whose best interest must we have at heart?

_____

_____

_____

3/According to verses 26-27, how long does the Lord give you to get rid of your anger? Why? What happens if resentment is *not* dealt with right away (Hebrews 12:15)?

---

note: The principle of not letting the sun go down on your anger can easily be taught to children by word and example. Let them know that in obedience to God, no one in your family ever goes to bed mad!

4/Describe the kind of communication that is pleasing to God. By contrast, describe the kind of communication that grieves the Holy Spirit (verses 29-32).

5/Should Christian parents overlook whining, temper tantrums, bickerng or unkind words? How should a parent handle these symptoms? Be specific.

---

note: A common philosophy is that people are naturally good. If you believe this, you won't see the need to train your children to be good. The Bible says we are all naturally sinful; that we need to put off the old nature and learn to put on the new (Ephesians 4:22-24).

6/Ephesians 1:12-13 says that those who have trusted Christ have been sealed by the Holy Spirit. What does verse 30 say about the Holy Spirit's sealing? What does a seal indicate? Is this true of you? How can you be sure?

"THINK ABOUT IT" QUESTIONS

note: Because the use of the tongue (communication) is a prominent theme in the book of Proverbs, we've selected several verses that are pertinent to communication in the family. James 3:1-12 also gives helpful wisdom on the use of the tongue.

Read aloud the following selected proverbs:

"Anxiety in a man's heart weighs him down, but a good word makes him glad." Prov. 12:25 (RSV)

"Pleasant words are like a honey-comb, sweetness to the soul and health to the body." Prov. 16:24 (RSV)

7/What is the topic of these proverbs? How can you verbally *encourage* your spouse and your children? Why is this important?

_____

"If one gives answer before he hears, it is his folly and shame." Prov. 18:13 (RSV)

"Good men think before they answer. Evil men have a quick reply, but it causes trouble." Prov. 15:28 (TEV)

8/What is the topic here? Do you take time to really *listen* to your spouse? To your children? Describe a good listener.

_____

Read aloud:

"Iron sharpens iron, and one man sharpens another." Prov. 17:17 (KJV)

"A good man's words are like pure silver; a wicked man's ideas are worthless." Prov. 10:20 (TEV)

9/Jesus tells us that our words reveal what is in our hearts (Matt. 12: 33-35.) List the most frequent topics of conversation in your home. Do these have a worthwhile "sharpening" effect on your family members?

_____

_____

10/What are some conversational topics that would be worthwhile?

What can you do to help your family conversation into constructive patterns?

_____

_____

Read aloud:

"He who is slow to anger is better than the mighty, and he who rules his spirit than he who takes a city." Prov. 16:32 (RSV)

"The start of an argument is like the first break in a dam; stop it before it goes any further." Prov. 17:14 (TEV)

"A soft answer turns away wrath, but a harsh word stirs up anger." Prov. 15:1 (RSV)

11/Meditate on the proverbs above before you answer these questions. Summarize what these proverbs teach about arguments. If you have a quick temper, what are some specific things you can do to control it? If someone in your family has a quick temper, how can you help him to cool down?

_____

_____

_____

Read aloud:

"Listen to advice and accept instruction, that you may gain wisdom for the future." Prov. 19:20 (RSV)

"A wise son hears his father's instruction, but a scoffer does not listen to rebuke." Prov. 13:1 (RSV)

12/Why, according to these proverbs, should we listen to advice? Why is criticism so difficult for us to accept?

_____

_____

"She opens her mouth with wisdom, and the teaching of kindness is on her tongue." Prov. 31:26 (RSV)

"Some people like to make cutting remarks, but the words of the wise soothe and heal." Prov. 12:18 (LB)

13/What is the best approach in *giving* advice? What should be the motive behind the giving of advice?

_____

_____

Read aloud:

"She is loud and stubborn." Prov. 7:11a (KJV)

"A foolish woman is noisy." Prov. 9:13a (RSV)

"A nagging wife is like water going drip-drip-drip." Prov. 19:13 (TEV)

"Better to live out in the desert than with a nagging, complaining wife." Prov. 21:19 (TEV)

14/Do you remember the woman described in I Peter 3 whose behavior is so precious in the sight of God? Contrast her with the foolish woman described in these proverbs.

_____

15/Why are the communications habits of a mother so important in a household? How do you define nagging? If this is your problem, why do you do it? How can you stop it?

_____

_____

Pray together now, mentioning specific communication problems to the Lord, and asking for His help for the coming week.

13

Luke 12:13-34
II Corinthians 9:9-15

Understanding God's view of material possessions:
THE CHRISTIAN FAMILY AND MONEY

Read Luke 12:13-16

1/What warning did Jesus give the two brothers who were arguing over their inheritance?

_____

note: Verse 15 is a good verse to memorize and repeat when Christmas shopping, spring house-cleaning, or any other time the temptation to be covetous strikes!

2/We live in a materialistic world. Christians, if they are not careful, can easily be influenced by the world's standards. Describe a materialistic family. Does this in any way describe your family?

_____

_____

3/What are some specific ways you can help your children to appreciate a simply, unmaterialistic way of life? What can you do to curb your own tendency to materialism?

_____

_____

Read Luke 12:16-21

4/What was the rich fool living for? Why was this short-sighted?

_____

5/Many passages in Scripture warn of the foolishness of making material possessions the goal of life. Paul tells us that "those who desire to be rich fall into temptation, into a snare, into many senseless and hurtful desires that plunge men into ruin and destruction." (I Tim. 6:9, RSV) What kind of wealth should we set our sights on (I Tim. 6:17, 18)? Are you encouraging your children to plan their lives with these objectives in mind?

_____

_____

Read Luke 12:22-34

6/What is Jesus warning us against—working for a living, or anxiety about money? (For added insight, see II Thessalonians 3:10-13.)

_____

7/God expects us to be responsible enough to provide for our families. He says, "If any provide not for his own, and specially for those of his own house, he hath denied the faith, and is worse than an infidel." (I Tim. 5:8, KJV) If this responsibility weighs heavily on your shoulders, how might Luke 12:28-31 be of comfort?

_____

8/Luke 12:31 is a well-known verse. Its counterpart in Matthew is even more familiar: "But seek ye first the kingdom of God, and his righteousness, and all these things shall be added unto you." (Matt. 6:33, KJV) What does this mean? Have you applied this promise to your life and experienced its truth? Explain.

_____

_____

Read II Corinthians 9:6-8

9/What happens to the person who is stingy in giving to the Lord? What happens to the person who is generous?

_____

10/Why do you think God loves cheerful generosity? What other guide-line for giving should we act on (Matthew 6:1-3)?

_____

11/In the Old Testament, believers who gave less than 10% were robbing God (See Malachi 3:8-10). How much should we give back to God today?

_____

Read II Corinthians 9:9-15

12/Verse 12 says that our giving helps meet the needs of the saints. Why is it important for Christians to be involved in supporting missionaries and evangelistic outreach ministries?

_____

13/How do you and your spouse decide where to give your money?

_____

note: Verse 13 says that our giving is an evidence of our faith. God wants us. Our gifts are simply an evidence of our love for Him. In II Corinthians 8:5 Paul tells how the Macedonians first gave themselves to God. Don't ask your spouse to give money to God if he hasn't first given him his life.

14/How should parents teach their children to give to the Lord?

_____

_____

15/What wonderful gift has God given to us (verse 15)?

_____

16/To whom do all of our possessions belong? How should this knowl-edge affect our attitude toward material possessions?

_____

_____

64

"THINK ABOUT IT" QUESTION

17/As a result of this study, do you see any changes that need to be made in your family financial patterns? What are they?

_____

_____

14

Building with God's instructions for:
DISCIPLINING OUR CHILDREN—PART I

note: The next two lessons will deal with discipline. We are using the word discipline *in its deepest sense to include not only chastening for bad behavior but training for good behavior.*

The central passage for these two lessons is Hebrews 12:5-15. This passage actually deals with God's discipline of believers. However, since parents are told to discipline as the Lord does, we believe this passage is definitely applicable to parents disciplining their children. We believe there is a connection between "disciplining" and "discipling," which is what Jesus did in training His followers.

These two lessons are at the end of this studyguide because many of the principles taught in the other lessons are fundamental to good discipline. If you have entered the study late, we especially recommend that you do lessons 9 and 12. Godly love and godly communication are fundamental to godly discipline.

Read Hebrews 12:5-8

1/What does the chastening of the Lord prove?

_____

2/Why is it a greater act of love to discipline a child than to always let him follow his own inclination?

_____

note: Proverbs 13:24 says "If you refuse to discipline your son, it proves you don't love him; for if you love him you will be prompt to punish him." (LB)

3/What lack does an unrestrained child sense that causes his parents' permissiveness? When a child tests boundaries we have set, what else is he also testing?

_____

4/According to the above proverb, broken rules call for prompt disciplinary action. How does the knowledge that God wants you to enforce your rules influence the standards you and your spouse set up for your children?

_____

note: You and your spouse would be wise to sit down together and decide which rules are important enough to enforce. Then stick to them!

5/Why is it better to discipline promptly than after the second or third offense? (Remember God's instructions about nagging in lesson 12.)

_____

Read Hebrews 12:9-11

6/Meditate on verse 9. When children learn to respect and obey their earthly fathers, whom else are they learning to obey?

_____

7/What is the end purpose of God's discipline according to this Hebrews passage? What should also always be your motive in disciplining your children?

_____

note: Proverbs 23:13, 14 says "Do not withhold discipline from a child; if you beat him with a rod, he will not die . . . you will save his life from Sheol." (RSV)

8/Explain the above proverb. How can the kind of discipline received in childhood affect a person's relationship with the Lord? What other authority figures is each individual likely to meet in life? How will respect for parents affect all relationships with authorities?

_____

_____

_____

9/Should discipline be administered in anger? (Remember God's instructions concerning anger in lesson 12.) Why, or why not?

_____

note: A spanking should be approached calmly, in love, and in obedience to God. Larry Christenson shares: "When I saw it was not my anger but God's Word which determined a spanking, I came to it in an entirely different spirit. Not in anger against the child, but in obedience to God. The whole atmosphere was different–and the children sensed it at once. The spankings were surer, harder–and fewer." Larry Christensen.[1]

10/There are many proverbs that tell us to use the rod as a means of discipline. Is the rod or its equivalent better than the hand? Why, or why not?

_____

11/Is discipline going to seem enjoyable at the time it is being administered (Hebrews 12:11)?

_____

note: Proverbs 19:18 says "Chasten thy son while there is hope, and let not thy soul spare for his crying." Because discipline is difficult for both parent and child, many of us are tempted to skip it. This shortcut is like building a house with hay and stubble–but it is really our children who will be unprepared in the time of testing.

12/What can a parent happily anticipate if he obeys God in disciplining his children (Hebrews 12:11)?

_____

note: Proverbs 29:17 says "Correct thy son, and he shall give thee rest; yea, he shall give delight unto thy soul." (KJV)

13/When your child is behaving responsibly, in obedience, do you think it's important to praise him? (Remember God's instructions concerning praise in lesson 12.) Why, or why not? How do you apply this?

_____

_____

[1]*Taken from* The Christian Family, © *1970, Bethany Fellowship. Used by permission.*

15

Building with God's instructions for:
DISCIPLINING OUR CHILDREN—PART II

note: For a better understanding of the context of this passasge, read the first eleven verses of this chapter–especially noting the first two. These verses tell Christians to run the race of life and to set aside any sins that would entangle them. Then in verse 12 they are told to strengthen weak hands and feeble knees. These would be weaknesses in their behavior that would slacken their pace in serving the Lord.

Read Hebrews 12:12-13

1/As parents, the behavior we should be concerned about correcting in our children is the behavior that is not pleasing to God. Each of us has "weak knees" and "lame legs" and "sins that easily entangle us". List some behavior in your own life that is not pleasing to God. (If you need help, see Exodus 20, Proverbs 6:16-19, Colossians 3:5-9, and II Timothy 3:1-5.)

_____

_____

_____

2/Some behavior in our children may not be displeasing to God but is irritating to us. (For example, spilling a glass of milk.) Can you think of another example? Is it fair to punish this kind of mistake?

_____

"THINK ABOUT IT" QUESTION

3/Ask the Lord to show you and your spouse the habits that He finds most displeasing in each of your children. Then ask Him to show you how to deal with it. (It might be kinder not to share this in a discussion group.)

_____

_____

note: Hebrews 12:13 reads "and make straight paths for your feet, so that the limb which is lame may not be put out of joint, but rather be healed." (NASV)

4/The habit of lying or swearing is a "crippling" factor in your child's life. Why, according to the verse above is it especially important for a parent to persevere in correcting this?

_____

note: Proverbs 22:6 says: "Train up a child in the way he should go and, when he is old, he will not depart from it." (KJV)

5/Hebrews 12:13 tells us to make straight paths for our feet. Why is it important to not only correct wrong behavior but to train a child in right behavior?

_____

note: The Lord tells the liar to stop lying and to start telling the truth. He tells the thief to stop stealing and to start making an honest living. He tells the critical tongue to stop saying unkind things and to start saying constructive, helplful things. (Ephesians 4:25-32)

6/How would you train your child in the following situations? (Remember, you need to not only stop the child from going on the wrong path but show him the right path.)

a) Your child is doing a sloppy job of a task you've given him—for example, making his bed.

_____

b) Your child is spending most of his free time watching worthless television programs.

_____

c) You hear your child teasing and being unkind to his brother.

Read Hebrews 12:14-15

7/Verse 14 tells us to strive for peace and holiness. Why is it especially important for the parent who is disciplining his children to be simultaneously leading a clean life, set apart for God?

"THINK ABOUT IT" QUESTION

8/Ask the Lord to show you, as a parent, if you have any "lame limbs" that need healing. Be still before Him. What is He showing you? What will you do about it?

9/Verse 15 warns against allowing any "root of bitterness" to spring up. Colossians 3:21 says "Fathers, do not exasperate your children that they lose heart." (NAS) What kind of discipline fits this description and leads to bitterness between child and parent? (If you are not sure—ask your children what they think is fair and unfair discipline.)

---

note: Ephesians 6:4 says: "And parents, never drive your children to resentment but in bringing them up correct them and guide them as the Lord does." (JB)

Consider the discipline of the Lord. His commands are clear and never heavier than we can bear. When we break His commands He chastens us because He loves us. His desire for us is that we become more like Christ. He shows no partiality and He is completely consistent. If we are repentant He is faithful and just to forgive us—completely and immediately. Because of His mercies we are not consumed. Great is His faithfulness!

10/As a parent, what insights have you gained into what it means to

God to be our Father? What has your experience of parenthood taught you that you could not have learned if you were childless?

_____

_____

notes

notes

notes

notes

notes

notes

notes